WHAT
MATTERS
MOST

WHAT MATTERS MOST

The Heart's Desires in Life and Death

Ann Bastianelli

This book was printed in the United States of America.

To contact Ann Bastianelli:

Ann Bastianelli
President
Anthology Consulting, Inc.
5124 North Pennsylvania Street, Suite 200
Indianapolis, Indiana 46205
www.anthologyconsulting.com
ann@anthologyconsulting.com

To order additional copies of this book, contact:
Xlibris Corporation
1-888-795-4274
www.Xlibris.com
Orders@Xlibris.com
21278

CONTENTS

PART II: WHAT TO DO

To all those who truly seek
to know what matters most and
then live by it

Acknowledgements

Many thanks to Andrea Marra, who kept my world in order during my time with Batesville and afterward, listening to my constant, excited revelations about what I was learning about life and death. She continues to provide perspective, nurturance, and atta-girls. My friend Larry Pitts encouraged me on this project and kept me going with calls, coffee and carryout. Lloyd Brooks and Sarah Branham, my colleagues at the Thrive Cooperative, guided the creative process on this book's cover design. Marlyn Wann handled the details of the manuscript format efficiently and with apparent joy. My editors Carolyn Lausch and Alex Boeglin read and made valuable comments on this manuscript in its making. As always, Dr. Mary Landy had faith in me.

I have gained inspiration for this work from my associations with my Indiana University faculty colleagues, John Earle and Terry Eccles of Arbor Memorial, Jim Price and Bob Horn of Keystone Group, Frank Stewart of Stewart Enterprises, Alan Creedy of Trust 100, John Hinger of Bolce Interior Image, Gene O'Grodnick, Dr. Alan Wolfelt, Dr. David Moller, Curt Zamec, Terry Whitlock, Mike Pazar, Allen Whitmer, and Julie Burn of Wilbert, Tony Colson, Mike DiBease, Keith Ashby, Jan Bell, Scott Billingsley, Dan Parker, Gary Hill, Gary Munchel, Floyd Hurley, and Bill Forsberg of Batesville. These people start and end each day ready, eager, and dedicated to creating new ways of delivering personal, poignant, humane service to humankind.

The following funeral service professionals operate their own outstanding firms and have been invaluable resources for me, providing key insights about this industry, the customers they serve, and their own vision: Lisa Baue, John Chasca, Patrick Downey, John Horan, Mark Musgrove, Mark Krause, Ernie Heffner, Bruce Buchanan, Mark Smith, and Mara Stuart.

Thanks to my family for their constant, loving support. And, especially to Christian, who knows he matters most to me.

Finally, thanks to God, for leading me, feeding me, and heeding me.

Preface

Trend tracking is situation assessment. Looking for trends involves a continual awareness of books, research and the media, including both traditional media such as newspapers, magazines, newsletters, TV news and radio broadcasts, and less traditional media such as Internet news sources, Websites, e-zines and billboards. All of these are methods marketers use to reach the public with marketing concepts, campaigns and educational information designed to address the deepest needs of their customers.

The better the marketers know their target customer, the more successfully the customer is reached with the right message. The best way to do that is to observe how they live, think, feel, act, and respond. I look for themes from society, business and culture that provide clues about what people's values are, how they feel about the cost of living, relationships, work, the rest of the world, and the meaning of it all.

I use consumer research as a starting point for developing my hypotheses. I also consider related industries that deal with the same consumers. I look at how consumers have responded to their messages and experiences for clues about what strategies, (whether accidental or intentional) have successfully connected with consumers' deepest needs. In the case of dealing with what I call the meaning of Life, the most obvious related industries are medicine & healthcare, organized religion, and funeral service.

Then, I conduct one-on-one interviews to discuss things with consumers, industry personnel and other experts outside of the industry. I ask lots of questions; aware that looking for patterns and trends is just as much art as science. The questions need to challenge as often as they confirm industry views and practices. Coming up with a clear picture of the future requires a blend of rhetoric and pragmatism. Trend spotting is *not* predicting the future.

Before ever addressing products and services, I need to understand what makes the users tick, how they see the world, and what the guiding principles are that form their opinions and buying decisions. In short, I focus on the state-of-mind benefits of using the products and services (the outside view) as opposed to what is missing functionally with them (the inside view).

Knowing about how people live provides clues about what their values are and how they will deal with Death and Funerals. And knowing that has allowed me to confidently draw implications and make recommendations to the funeral service industry, so that their products and services can become a more valued element of consumers' lives. I identify what I think is probably going to happen in the personal and business realms of life, and then speculate on the implications to funeral service if it does.

You can keep my roadmap to the future, design your own route based on it, or discard it and operate without any navigational aids. My view of the future gives you destinations and then provides information on what I think you will see on the way there. Then, it suggests what to do to arrive first, if you want to.

This book is a response to your requests. Every time I talk about this research, I am asked when I am speaking next, and where my books can be purchased. I recently was asked to emcee a birthday party for two women who invited their women friends to attend, learn about, and talk about the meaning of life. Following one of my speeches to a national convention, one enthusiastic audience member called this information a roadmap to the future.

Ann Bastianelli, Summer 2004

Introduction

Ann vibrantly engages the issues of grief and loss as life lessons. Her message—critically important to those who serve bereaved persons—is presented with unparalleled lucidity, good humor, and a deep sense of humanity. There has never been a more urgent time in our nation's history to listen to her voice and pay attention to her insights. She is a refreshing and innovative thought-leader in a vitally important profession.

Dr. David Moller,
Director of Medical Humanities, University of
Missouri-Kansas City School of Medicine

Part I
Life Trends

Chapter 1

Matters of Life and Death

To put it mildly, my friends and family were surprised when I decided to work in the funeral service industry, or, as I like to call it, the 'Meaning of Life' industry.

"You are going to do *what?*"

There was a method to what they saw as my madness, though. I had previously worked for Franklin-Covey as a facilitator of two courses, *Seven Habits of Highly Effective People,* and *First Things First.* In a nutshell, these courses help participants appreciate the importance of leading a purposeful life. This material is so compelling that invariably every participant sees value in defining their life mission and leading their life so that at its end, they can be certain that they had an unmistakable impact on the people and things they cared about most. Common sense would dictate that the opposite way of living (randomly and directionless, reacting to one Life event after another) is not an option anyone would choose. Common sense is not common practice, though. Fewer than 7% of the world's population have ever thought about or written down their mission, much less lived by it. I had enjoyed coaching people on achieving what they determined to be their life's purpose.

When I got a call from a headhunter about a position at Hillenbrand Industries as head of marketing for Batesville Casket Company, I was intrigued with the prospect of studying Life's purpose and meaningfulness retrospectively from another angle, the viewpoint of the dying and their families. When all was said and done, did people really accomplish their life's purpose? What *really* mattered to people at Life's end?

Having accepted the position of Director of Marketing for Batesville, the world's largest manufacturer of caskets and urns, I understood my role to be to identify funeral-related products, services, ideas, and innovations that would strike a successful chord with consumers. What would the primary motivators of the 21st century consumer be for these kinds of products and services? What could be done so that people could see greater value in having a funeral? Was it possible to improve the experience of death? How could the funeral be improved? What did the families of the dying expect from the funeral director and others?

I was curious about the death care industry as a marketing communications challenge, too. If it were possible to generate consumer interest in funerals, what would be the best way to do it? Would people want to learn about funerals?

I had never planned a funeral for a loved one. I didn't know what it felt like to handle a myriad of details while coping with my own feelings of loss. I didn't know whom I'd trust to ask for help. Truly, I didn't even know what questions I'd have. So, I approached this challenge the way I have every other marketing challenge I've faced. I completely immersed myself in the consumer experience, becoming aware of, shopping for, selecting, using and judging the efficacy of all the products and services available. In this case, I immersed myself in anything and everything related to Death, dying, funerals, and the Meaning of Life.

One of my first calls was to Dr. David Moller, an author, expert, and professor of Death & Dying at Indiana University. At the time, Dr. Moller was also the chairman of the Program in Medical Humanities and Medical Ethics at Indiana University Medical Center. I told Dr. Moller what my position was at Batesville, and that I needed to understand what it was like to be dying. I wanted to understand, from the moment a person receives a terminal diagnosis, through their illness, death and funeral, how Life changed. Who helped them? Who served their needs? Was it the medical community? The clergy? The funeral director? Was it somebody I hadn't even imagined? *What Really Mattered?*

Dr. Moller was intrigued with this idea because, as a faculty member in the Palliative Care Program at the I.U School of Medicine, he was dedicated to palliative care and helping people die with dignity and in as much comfort as possible. His view was that my internship and the perspective I would bring from the Death Care industry would help doctors better understand the thought processes, fears, and desires of their terminal patients and their families. Together, he thought, we could do things that would improve death, dying, and funeral experiences.

Throughout the internship, I observed, investigated and analyzed human behavior and desires, academically, theoretically and pragmatically, in the laboratory of the real world. I was completely changed, both personally and professionally as a result. Hearing the personal stories of the dying, I was able to add human truths to the stacks of inanimate product knowledge already available to the industry. I brought this information about consumer desires back to those who could respond to it. Not just to Batesville, but also to funeral directors, doctors, nurses, clergy and community leaders who hadn't seen anything like this before. Standing alongside the dying, I could make unique observations and relay consumer desires and questions about products, services, environments and experiences. Everything deserved to be revisited, from products themselves, to how they were merchandised, to how funerals are planned and conducted. What I learned became the basis for whole new strategies designed to address consumers' deepest needs and desires when it comes to end-of-life decisions, memorialization, and funerals.

The more I studied how society copes with death, the more evident it became: *The business of dying makes the human experience of it more painful, rather than less.* It seemed obvious that the medical community, organized religion and the funeral profession all served the same customer: dying persons and their families. The business models of these industries, however, don't match up well with the human reality of dying and death. This makes it difficult, if not impossible, for them to meet the deepest, most personal human needs of their customers.

Today, the dying process is analogous to a relay: It's a hand-off from one expert to the next. Experts are involved only for the brief time in which a family deals with them, for decisions about a surgical procedure, a sacrament, ceremony, or funeral. A better option would be a cooperative, collaborative model of service providers whose offerings change with each family.

As long as these industries remain compartmentalized into discrete businesses, the business of death will continue to operate with its inside-out model. I was examining Life and Death from *outside* the industry, and from *inside* the hearts and minds of the families enduring it. From that vantage point, I learned that the things that follow are those that matter most.

Death and funerals resurrect Life in a way nothing else can. In so doing, they clarify one's purpose for living and roles in Life.

There are two aspects of suffering. The first is that there is virtue in misery. It's an awful truth that suffering can deepen us, making the luster of our colors greater and the resonance of our words richer. If optimism and spirit remain, then the capacity for vision and appreciation for simple, indispensable, transcendent things does, too. The second aspect of suffering is that there are a surprising number of things to be learned in suffering that are, for some reason, impossible to learn any other way.

There are four things a person needs both during Life and at Life's End. The first is people with whom to share their concerns. It is important to be socially integrated and part of a larger, stronger group that provides support and sustenance. The second is people who are dependable in a pinch. This ensures that you will receive help even if you don't know how to ask for it. These are friends who know *intuitively* what you need and can speak for you, or step in for you. The third is close friends. True emotional intimacy reaches deep into our souls. And, truly, actions proving our connection to others speak louder than words. The fourth thing people need is others who respect them and believe in their worth as a human *being*, not as a human *doing*. No matter what happens, these people know your true worth. They see you for who you are, and love you for who you are.

The most comforting things that should be said *frequently* in Life, and *finally*, at Life's End are:

> "I forgive you."
> "Will you forgive me?"
> "Thank you."
> "I love you."
> "Goodbye and farewell."

The things that matter are Forgiveness, Gratitude, Love, Faith and Hope.

The experience a person has with dying is not the same as the clinical pathology of the disease they are dying from. Those who are actively dying are hoping to achieve a *Good* Death. To them, this means dying in a way that will transform their dying into a final opportunity for self-enhancement, growth, and an inspired quest for meaning.

In contemplating funerals, memorial ceremonies, or tributes after death, the dying universally agree to these expectations for their funerals.

➤ The funeral should reflect the way they lived, what they stood for, and the person they became.

➤ The family should be recognizable as their loved ones, so that those attending will know immediately who to provide support to.

➤ The funeral should provide a sense of peace, hope, and the transcendence of fear. Their hope is that the feelings of fatigue, vulnerability and anxiety brought on by their chronic illness will begin to be eased by the energy, fellowship, and vitality of group worship.

➤ The funeral should organize the 'grieving period, gently presenting the new social order of the family and providing a connection to past family traditions. It should also legitimize the reason for getting together. There is comfort in numbers.

➤ The funeral should confirm the reality: This family has lost a member. The visible presence of the body focuses attention on that reality and, by preventing denial, lets even greater more authentic expressions of sympathy and grief occur.

➤ The funeral should motivate the family and other mourners to appreciate Life, affirm their own existence, and find personal meaning.

➤ The funeral should provide an opportunity for the grieving network' to express itself in an organized way. It is the time and place in which individual self-expression can serve as a coping mechanism in death's immediate aftermath.

➤ The funeral should invite informal, familiar, comfortable ways of interacting into a setting that may seem uncomfortable: the funeral home. Anything that can be done should be done to make the funeral home more like the family home.

➤ The funeral should provide tangible evidence of the love, support and concern of friends through the traditional sending of flowers. Even though some feel that sending flowers is not practical, or that the money could be used more wisely, this custom is an important symbol of the support of the community, and as such, makes a lasting impression on the family.

From my point-of-view, the more I learned, the more I wanted to know, and the more convinced I became that the experience of death, dying, and memorialization could be much better than it is. In American society today, the typical response to the 'problem' of death is to 'solve' it by managing it technologically. Dying persons are offered ways of dying that are 'socially dignified'. Then, they are offered a 'socially dignified' funeral. Personal preferences about these two important experiences, the death and the funeral, are often ignored. In fact, when dying people hear the words 'dignified death' and 'dignified funeral' they know it to mean dying without causing public distress to the *non-dying*. It is almost as if the difficulty of dying, Death itself, and planning a funeral are being ignored completely and replaced by less socially disruptive alternatives.

Death and funerals resurrect Life like nothing else can. They can clarify our purpose for living and point out what really matters. In short, they can teach us how to live well. Dying leads to conversations about Age, Longevity, Extremism & Simplicity, Loss and Healing, Funerals, Storytelling, Security and Mistrust, Spirituality, and God, among other things. This book is about our deepest human desires for living, dying, and memorialization. It reveals what is possible, probable and preferable at Life's End, and recommends what funeral service can do to make what's preferable a certainty.

Chapter 2

Age & Power

Michelangelo said, "The greatest danger for most of us is not that our aim is too high and we miss it, but that it is too low, and we hit it."

In generations past, people didn't age. They died. There will never be an end to death. But both life and death continue to change so dramatically, the 'Meaning of Life' industries would do well to raise their aim when it comes to serving customers.

Ever since Mick Jagger turned 50 years old, the world had to rethink what old age meant. Now, when you ask a 50 year olds when they think old age begins, they're likely to answer, 'Eighty.' In America, the most desired age is the median age: 36. It's also is the new favorite age of power. Some call this stage mid-*youth*, not middle *age*. Either way, it lasts until menopause starts. Mid-youth is Demi Moore. Mid-youth is also Marilyn Monroe. It's Princess Diana. It's experience, enthusiasm and excitement. And, it's hot.

Due to advances in medicine, sanitation, wellness programs, food science, pharmacology, and healthier lifestyles, the current life expectancy of 77 years is thirty years more than it was at the last turn of the century. According to *The New York Times*, the greatest miracle in the history of humanity is the doubling of life expectancy since the start of the Industrial Age. Our odds of overcoming any medical problem are so good that the average 46 year old living in America, the U.K., Germany, or Japan today can count on having a 100th birthday. Some experts believe a baby born today will have a life expectancy of 115 to 120 years old.

The most intriguing implication about increased life expectancy is the fastest growing demographic segment: People 85 and older. By 2050, nearly one out of five people is going to be *at least* 85 years old. Imagine how different Life will be when every fifth person you meet will be 85 or older. For the next generation, that will be the reality.

Already people 65 and older, traditionally referred to as elders, make up 27% of the population in America, and 36% of all adults. Elders own 70% of all the wealth. They are 66% of all stockholders, and own 40% of all mutual funds, and 60% of all annuities. They own 38%, or $34 billion in life insurance, and 90% of all long-term care insurance policies, worth $800 million in annual premiums. Elders account for $610 billion in healthcare spending. They own almost half of the credit cards issued in the United States.

Government entitlements, home ownership, saving and investing throughout life, along with senior discounts on everything from travel and entertainment to financial services, have helped shove the official poverty rate for elders to an all time low. Elders also make up the 32 million members of AARP, which is the number one lobbying organization in the United States, and the second largest not-for-profit organization behind the Catholic Church.

According to Ken Dychtwald, author of *Age Wave*, there are four outcomes certain to result from this powerful new "gerontocracy":

- ➢ More people will be living longer than ever before.
- ➢ Their behavior will be their biggest challenge.
- ➢ Economic and Political power will shift to the elders.
- ➢ Different thinking will exist about how to spend those unexpected extra years.

Add to increased longevity the fact that there were 30% fewer babies being born in the U.S. between the years of 1925 and 1930, and the conclusion is inescapable: It's a great time to be alive! Growth in the death rate isn't likely over the next decade. By the looks of it, we're going to be alive a good long while, so it makes sense for us to give some thought to living well.

Chapter 3

Extremism vs. Simplicity

Today, living well usually involves balancing two opposing impulses. The first is a focus on 'having it all' in the most extreme, exciting way possible. It's leading a full, flexible, diverse life. It's multitasking for the thrill of it. It works like this. You figure, "Hey, as long as I have to travel, I might just as well take my wife and kids with me. It may be the only way we'll be able to take a family vacation this year." (This is much better than canceling out on your family year in and year out because of your anxiety about taking vacation days, appearing uncommitted professionally, and worrying the whole time about losing your job.) So you take your family with you when you travel to those continuing education classes at places like The Disney Institute or the Hyatt. Even if you have to pay the family's way while your boss pays yours, everybody wins. Your boss gets a trained, refreshed employee, you get professional renewal and the love and gratitude of your family, and the family gets a vacation.

The goal of this first method of living well is to sample all Life has to offer by leading a spontaneous, stimulating, exciting life. Think of it as a Chinese menu approach, browsing Life's buffet in search of optimal state-of-mind. Melinda Davis, futurist and CEO of the Next Group, calls this 'The State of O' (short for Optimal State-of-Mind), a place inside us reserved for peak experiences and healing bliss. Some people talk about Synchronicity in referring to 'O'. Some call it "The Zone". To others, it is "Going with the Flow:, the "Runner's High", or being "In the Groove". 'O' is the ultimate reward for living the Life of our Dreams. "The State of O" makes us feel most alive and least overwhelmed. The pursuit of 'O' is not limited to a religious or spiritually defined goal, but can also include a desire for peak experiences of the imagination, even ones that last momentarily.

The second way to live well involves an opposing impulse to the first. It is a search for a simpler, more controllable life. Too much sensory stimulation in Life has created a need for many of us to find a way to simplify it all. It's hard to turn down the volume, take control, and reclaim your personal space. No wonder 82% of those responding to a recent poll said that 'a quiet place of meditation and reflection' is the number one new 'must have' for their home. In the meantime, we wade through inescapable disruption and craziness daily.

Already in 1999, 12% of Americans had joined a voluntary simplicity movement in an effort to reduce their stress, according to *Fast Company* magazine. A study done in 2000 at the University of California Berkeley revealed that the world is producing 250 megabytes of non-repetitive new data to add to our existing mind traffic each year.

Is all this information really necessary?

Consumers don't want more choices. They want a reasonable number of options. Putting the choices into packages of some kind would help. Less complicated products would help. It's the desire for simplicity that is behind consumer interest in companies and individuals that organize and categorize issues, ideas, products and services, remove the complexity of them, and package them in assortments that make sense.

Americans seek simplicity every chance they get. Most of us have already tried escaping to a simpler time by delegating the right to decide what will entertain and relax us to TV networks. Unfortunately, researchers studying the effects of increased TV viewing reveal that more viewing does not, in fact, relax one's mind by decreasing & simplifying mental activity. TV merely pushes different buttons.

Maybe that's why, in the 1990's, when overworked, overstressed people had little time for television, the most popular program for seven years was Seinfeld, which according to its creators, was based on 'nothing'. That was its appeal, the relief it promised and delivered.

Today, society's tastes have boomeranged to a preoccupation with physical survival and overachievement. When watching TV doesn't relax us, we turn to extreme thrills, continuing our search for optimal state-of-mind. With things like bungee jumping and extreme sports, we seek the element of surprise. On a deeper level, though, we are on the prowl for immersive stimulation so we can escape our real life reality.

The networks drew people back to TV with reality programming that allowed viewers to experience life on the edge from the safety & comfort of their family rooms. The participants in these shows have been dunked in a whole new world and left to try to cope. Survivalism takes us back to the days of the Spartans, when human fears were simply about Man vs. Nature. Reality show fans believe that that there are so many truly scary things happening today, physical survival isn't even an issue anymore! Maybe the hair-raising situations faced by reality players makes us feel more able to handle the simpler situations life hands us daily.

More than challenging viewers' survival instincts, 'Extreme Makeover', and 'The Swan' suggest that merely being who your DNA dictated is not enough to attract 'The Average Joe'. This has caused great anxiety about heredity and humdrum lives.

Not that we need more anxiety. It's just that we don't think we can improve ourselves on our own. Enter the fastest growing area in pharmaceuticals: *lifestyle* pharmaceuticals. These do anything from enhancing sex-drive and performance to relieving anxiety and depression, to adjusting negative body image and bruised self-esteem, to handling social phobias.

In summary, the goal of living well is to achieve an optimal state-of-mind we can depend on to guide every aspect of our lives. And, this important goal tends to be pursued in either of two divergent methods, by seeking a full, flexible, diverse life, and extreme experiences, or by seeking a simpler life that turns down the volume.

Chapter 4

Playing Hard

Recreation is the fastest growing area of per capita consumption among Americans. This is right in line with the human desire for a full, flexible, diverse life. More than Human *Beings*, we are Human *Doings*. Once we've mastered our day-to-day routines, we want variety. Or, at least we think we do.

When your teenage daughter asks, "Dad, would you take me to the mall with my friends?" it's very difficult to muster the energy you think you need to comply with her request. You don't want to go to the mall. You've been working a long day and this will make it even longer. The only thing you really want to do is collapse in front of the TV. Instead, you give yourself a good talking to. You love your daughter. It's important to demonstrate that you are a good dad. There must be something for you to do at the mall! Sure, there is. Retailers know how hard it is to find time to shop. So, they're trying to make it worthwhile by making it fun for everyone. So, when you get to the mall there *are* some things designed with you in mind. For instance, you can have a water massage, right there in the mall with your clothes on! You just wiggle into one of those jumbo tubes and have a water jet massage!

This is a new state-of-mind benefit of shopping, isn't it? You get a therapeutic massage that you wouldn't have gotten otherwise, and your daughter and her girlfriends get to shop. It's a win-win scenario in which everybody achieves their own idea of recreation, their own state of 'O'. An added benefit: all of your daughter's friends are telling her how great a dad you are because you consented to do something their parents refused to! Through 2010, consumers are going to continue to spend more on recreation, while spending more on fitness, healthcare & wellness.

Chapter 5

The New Collectible: Experiences

What qualifies as recreation is highly dependent on who you talk to. Everyone seems to agree, though, that living creatively means you are *doing* things, and in the process, adding to your life experiences. At Life's End, people talk about *the things they did or did not do*, not what they *have*.

The appeal of collecting experiences is that they are unable to be saved up or stored. Experience collectors revel in the fact that what they have is something desirable, intangible and priceless. They live for the feeling of having been treated to an enviable experience someone felt they deserved. It's the difference between receiving a surprise 40th birthday party and a once-in-a-lifetime trip to Old St. Andrews Golf Club in Scotland, or getting a fancy new suit. No contest. Old St. Andrews is lasting in its effect and demonstrates that the giver has intimate knowledge of something that really matters to you (golf). This trip will be a highlight of your life because it was out-of-the-ordinary, and priceless in a way that defies description. Besides, the value was in *your having been there to experience it first-hand*. It's easy to understand why experiences are so valued by consumers today. We are a materialistic society with far too many things we just don't need. We don't need more *things*. Besides, conventional gifts are quickly forgotten.

The social currency of the moment is experience value. In their book, *The Experience Economy*, Joseph Pine and James Gilmore outline the evidence that ours is a society partial to, and prepared to pay for, experiences. The Experience Economy is the industrial market's response to the consumer described earlier, the one whose paradoxical is a balancing act between a jam-packed, spontaneous, 'having it all' existence, and a simpler, easier-to-control life.

Four realms of experience exist. The first is the educational realm, which addresses our intellectual need for efficiency and mental stimulation. People's goal is to learn from these types of experiences. The second is the entertainment realm, which serves our emotional need for nurturing and self-esteem. The goal of these types of experiences is to move people to *feel*. The clearest examples of this is movies, which can compel us to cry, laugh, be frightened, or feel all of these things! The third is the esthetic realm of experience, which serves our spiritual need for fulfillment and freedom. The appeal of the esthetic experience is evident in the new popularity of yoga. Over the past half-decade the number of yoga classes in U.S. health clubs has nearly doubled. Exercising the mind, body, and spirit is difficult, yet in a way that's more appealing than a frenetic, sweaty, muscle-burning workout. Yoga multi-tasks by simultaneously healing mind, body and soul, saving time and multiplying pleasure. The fourth and final realm is the escapist realm, which serves our physical need to do things that conveniently bring us comfort, exhilaration and pleasure. Bungee jumping, chat rooms, video games, gambling, and even recreational drug use are experiences in this realm.

Experiences that are most memorable usually involve several of these realms. In fact, the more an experience services our intellectual, emotional, spiritual, and physical needs, the more distinctive and memorable it is. For instance, the esthetic and escapist realms of experience are being combined more and more often in response to studies showing that hospital patients who had rooms with views of beautiful landscapes or gardens had shorter post-operative stays and required less pain medication than those who didn't. The healing gardens now being built by businesses, homeowners and funeral homes are leveraging the proven healing power of botanical, pastoral pleasure.

Chapter 6

Making Memories

We want a life that's interesting enough to be truly memorable. There are three things necessary to upgrade any ordinary occasion to a memorable one: Surprise, Indulgence, and Souvenirs.

Think about the birthdays you remember. Part of what made them memorable was that something unexpected happened. It might have been excessive in some way: food, decorations, gifts, or guests. After a party like that, you wanted proof it happened. You wanted to remember it. You wanted to preserve memories, through pictures, movies, goodie bags, or souvenirs.

If you've ever been to a Disney resort, you've seen this equation of surprise, indulgence, and souvenirs in action. You spend $3,000 on a vacation. Then, on the last day, when you've run completely through your vacation budget, on the way to the exit, in the last 500 yards you spend another $300 on Mickey Mouse ears and tee shirts. You do this so that when you get home you can put on the tee shirt and people will ask, "Did you go to Disney?" You buy souvenirs and indulgences to make experiences last as long as possible and to preserve memories so that you can reminisce and relive your favorite moments in Life. You enjoy telling stories about these memories. Others know, by listening to you, that you live well.

McDonald's restaurants have made a science out of creating a memorable experience for every child that enters. Nothing is left to chance. First, they determine the themes for the Happy Meals for the year. Then, they build their products, services, and promotional experiences around the theme for each month. When these themes borrow interest & value from the movie industry, with a Winnie the Pooh Happy Meal, for instance, the excitement and fun is multiplied. When the Pooh movie is promoted via a McDonald's Happy Meal, it's difficult to tell which does more to gain the attention of the child target—the Happy Meal or the movie itself. McDonald's and its agencies invent Happy Meal toys appropriate to the theme, making sure that they have strong 'play-value' for kids. The simple objective is to engage all five senses of the pint-sized kid target. The ads must be fun and colorful to watch and listen to, the food must be fresh and hot, and kids' treatment at the stores must be unmatched by competitors, so that the kids will encourage their parents to bring them back. This formula works time after time. Here, too, the success formula involves surprise, indulgence and souvenirs.

Chapter 7

What vs. How

For decades, the DeBeers Diamonds campaign promised, "Diamonds are forever." When that ad campaign began, it was about permanence, and the diamond was the symbol of the promise of the eternal commitment of marriage. The permanence of the diamond itself was shorthand for the eternal durability of relationships. Today, diamonds may last forever, but relationships often don't.

It used to be that when a young woman got engaged, she wanted to show off her ring. Then, weddings were about the tangible evidence of a ring as a measure of commitment: the bigger the ring, the better the catch. 'Better' meant how much he loved her, and what his long-term earning potential was.

Today, when a couple gets engaged, the big questions are whether there are any unique aspects of the wedding festivities, and where the honeymoon is going to be. It's *how you are treated rather than what you got*. It's these intangible things that are clues to the kind of people the bride and groom are. Take the wedding. Is the couple going to be married At Wrigley Field? At Disney World? It may sound odd, but these locations may be far more emblematic of the personalities of the couple than the local Baptist Church. Now, look at the honeymoon plans. Whether the couple is going on safari or going to Peoria for the Annual Toothpick Festival says a lot about them.

You get the idea. *Everybody* gets a wedding ring, so it doesn't mean what it once did. The ring is a formality of the wedding ceremony: the tangible evidence of the marriage vows. Choose a different kind of wedding ceremony, and the relative importance of the ring changes. Consumers used to put far more emphasis on material goods, but seem to be trying to distance themselves now. They certainly do at the end of their lives. *Things* don't matter.

Permanence and durability used to be what sold products like DeBeers diamonds and gave them value. Ironically, there is a parallel between the declining importance of both the wedding rings at a wedding ceremony and the casket at a funeral. You don't *have* to have a casket to have a funeral. Caskets are merely a customary formality of a traditional funeral ceremony. If you don't want a traditional funeral, then the importance of the casket can be debated. A non-traditional funeral (sometimes called a Celebration of Life today) might focus on something people feel is more personal and meaningful to them such as a very special personal ritual, the visitation, the reception following, or a special tribute at the gravesite.

Years ago, marketing exchanges were all about the product. Now they are about service. This is true of most areas of life. How much we are willing to pay for something has everything to do with what we want it to *do* for us: what its *function* is. Its dollar value equates to how substantial its functional features and benefits are, and how important those things are to us personally. In other words, if Price is about *function*, then Value is about *substance*.

The implication for marketers is clear. Beyond their basic function, what substantial benefits do your products offer? Preferably the benefits should be about helping customers attain optimal state-of-mind. Be careful of overvaluing guarantees as a benefit. We consumers *expect* the things we buy to work. Otherwise, we would not have purchased them. You must guarantee what you sell. *A marketing exchange isn't a bet* between the consumer and provider. *It is a promise* of function and value. Today, consumers' self-images are formed by how they are treated and what they are entitled to in exchange for their hard earned dollars. Knowing what is of substantial value to your customers is critical to making your product and service offerings desirable.

Anyone who has paid for a wedding lately knows that the current average cost is, well, higher than you might think. The average cost of a wedding has grown 50% in the past decade, from $15,208 in 1990 to $22,360 in 2002, according to the Conde Nast Bridal Infobank. Their study also found that 43 percent of couples said they spent more on the wedding than they had planned. What a surprise.

Whether one has a wedding, however, does not hinge on one's ability to stomach the cost. Weddings are about buying the orchestration of the fairytale experience promised to a little girl years earlier. Wedding value is not about the *function* of the wedding, to be legally married. If it were, less expensive alternatives that result in the legal marriage of two people would be far more popular. No, what justifies the investment in a wedding is its value in publicly expressing the caring between parents and children and a man and woman. You are buying the intangible, emotional expression of love. The wedding itself becomes a defining Life experience. Notice the comments of wedding guests sometimes:

> "Hey this is some party, isn't it?"
> "I didn't know this about Bob. He's really got pretty good taste."
> "He looks as good as I've ever seen him."
> "What a wonderful family."

The wedding you buy says a lot about you and your family. It is a great communicator. It is a comment on your ability to live well. Funerals can be all of those things too, *and for all the same reasons.*

Chapter 8

It's all in your mind

In this virtual, 'imaginational' age, the body has been demoted to second-class status. An old religious concept had maintained that the body was superfluous—a vessel for the deeper truth inside it. This idea is spreading again like a virus through the culture and is already mainstream in the arts. The mind even rules the physical world. We control computers with brain waves that combine words, phrases and sentences to communicate, using only the power of our imagination. We do videoconferences and play virtual games and cyber-sports. It's all in our minds.

The lure of the imagination as our ally in Life is powerful. Thirty million Americans seek faith healers and alternative therapies each year. Seventy-seven percent of us believe God intervenes to cure the seriously ill. Half of U.S. medical schools teach their students about the importance of faith in successful healing. Two-thirds of the studies done on remote healing say it works. The mind, and specifically prayer and directed spiritual energy, has a powerful effect on medical outcomes. This tangible evidence of the power of the mind takes on a whole new significance when our bodies are under attack from disease and Death.

"Life hasn't been about the body for a long, long time," said a retail expert participating in a think tank discussing the wholeness of the body. "Get over it (the body)" said the August 2001 issue of *Wired* Magazine, "We have better things to take its place."

No wonder cremation is becoming so popular. Who needs a body?

Chapter 9

Lots more information than learning

Society has more information than ever but often is overwhelmed rather than enriched by it. Our economy involves commercial exchanges and is dependent on information. Every day, new methods of getting more information are introduced, yet consumers' tried-and-true methods of learning about what's happening in the world haven't changed substantially.

The glut of information has not added to our collective knowledge of things that matter. In fact, for most people, the increase in available information just makes them more aware that they probably don't have the very latest, most comprehensive knowledge on any topic. This adds to the stress and uncertainty they feel when making product and service decisions.

Consumers have no way to judge the value of the information they receive on end-of-life issues, be it on medical or funeral matters. For instance, making funeral arrangements typically occurs once every fifteen years. In effect, each time you plan a funeral, it's as if it were your first time. If you had planned a funeral years earlier after enduring the loss of a loved one, you wouldn't recall many details of the planning. And even if you did all those years later, those details wouldn't help much. Today's most memorable funerals have become *events,* and in some cases multimedia *experiences.* Things have changed.

Every death is tragic. No matter whose it is or how it happened. For this reason, decisions made when planning a funeral are primarily for peace-of-mind and answer these questions:

'How will my family feel when it is over?'
'Will it make me feel better?'
'What will my friends and the rest of the community say?'

'Will it be fitting?'

'Will the funeral provide peace and comfort?'

'Will it give us some sense of closure?'

Not surprisingly, there is a growing interest in learning more about dealing with end-of-life issues such as dying, medical directives, wills, trusts, lasting legacies, and funeral planning. It's just that people don't know whom to trust to teach them about these things. In February of 2000, the front page of the *Wall Street Journal* ran an article which began with this quote, "Convinced that the funeral industry, organized religion and the medical establishment fail to provide spiritual, fulfilling, or intimate deaths, professionals calling themselves Death Guides are stepping in."

Baby Boomers have allowed, encouraged, and are patronizing these 'Death Guides' whose goal is to accompany the dying person through the dying process, helping him or her to find meaning and resonance in a time so filled with pain and hopelessness. These professionals educate the dying on what things are going to happen and, when necessary, refer them to others on financial, economic, social, spiritual, and community issues related to dying. They facilitate the process of death, its location, the attendees, any ritual desired, and the degree of medical assistance requested by the dying person. In these important ways, Death Guides are meeting consumers' need for peace-of-mind and some control over these very personal matters.

Elsewhere, in response to demand for this type of learning, University of California at Santa Cruz, Duke University, Indiana University and countless others offer courses on how to prepare for Death, including how to plan funerals. In fact, during my internship, I took the Death and Dying course at Indiana. Enrollees included medical interns, nurses, funeral directors, clergy, chaplains, college students who had lost their parents, elders, and me, the Director of Marketing for the world's largest casket manufacturer. There was a waiting list to register for this class. I understand that the interest in this topic is so high, there is a waiting list *every* semester.

The popularity and demand for courses like this one suggests that although the general population is better educated than previous generations, they are not more knowledgeable about Life and Death matters. Certainly, because they have attended fewer funerals than their ancestors, the general population doesn't have much experience with such things. Faced with planning a funeral for a loved one, most Baby Boomers don't know where to begin. They refer to the few experiences they have had as attendees of funerals in which they used the opportunity to role-rehearse and informally plan their own.

A significant number of Boomers have been strongly influenced by a society that is mourning-avoidant and efficiency-based. The world they live in believes faster is better, and funerals only make people feel worse. And, since so many of the funerals Boomers have attended have been generic, even impersonal, there is a danger that, in increasing numbers, they will begin to see more value in saving money than in investing in a funeral of any kind.

Most families believe it's a good idea to understand each other's wishes in advance and spare one another the burden of planning a funeral when a death occurs. Still, they resist initiating funeral pre-planning conversations. One ironic example of this comes to mind. Over an 18-month period, TV Journalist Bill Moyers researched and produced a documentary called *Death and Dying*, which ultimately aired to great critical acclaim in the fall of 2000. When interviewed about his own end-of-life plans, however, Moyers was embarrassed to admit that, although his son had asked him repeatedly to have a conversation about it, he "just couldn't do it."

Chapter 10

Society Struggles with Death

Harold Kushner, the rabbi laureate of Temple Israel in Natick, Massachusetts, and author of *When Bad things Happen to Good People* has said, "Tragedy has no meaning. We give it meaning by the way we respond."

Maybe the time has come for funeral service professionals to broaden their vision to include helping people find meaning in the tragic experience of dying. We die the way we live. Until we die, all we know how to do is live. It makes sense, then, to look at the four prevalent societal values that impact our ability to deal with death. They are Materialism, Secularism, Technocism, and Individualism.

Let's look at each of these in turn. First, Materialism. Think about the life-long messages we receive from parents, teachers, coaches, and well-meaning friends, "You can achieve whatever you want, you can have whatever you wish, as long as you work hard enough." And so, perhaps because society has collectively internalized that message, society measures the worth of people by what they have, by what they own, by where they live, by what car they drive, or by whether or not their spouse is good looking. Material possessions provide a lot of information about a person to a curious (nosy) society.

Society judges our material worth before it judges us. At the moment you are given a terminal diagnosis, the reality registers that you will soon forfeit all your material wealth: your spouse, your kids, your home, your lake cottage, the country club, and finally, your body. The dying understand at that instant, that no matter what riches they may have accumulated on Earth, in Money, Possessions, Connections, or Relationships, we all return to God alone, armed only with the manner in which we lived. As a community of human beings in search of the meaning of Life, we understand that society's materialistic scorecard is irrelevant when finally we face Death, but that has not slowed the tendency of society to continue to measure us by our possessions rather than our personhood.

The lavishness of Life is lost to Death. It is an old, but true saying: *You can't take it with you.* Death is the Decomposition of One's Material Life.

Secondly, Secularism. We are a secular society. Gallup reports that only 34% of Americans say they attend worship services once weekly, a number that has not changed in ten years. Additionally, some who *do* worship say they are turned off by organized religion lately because of clergy scandals or overly vocal leadership on contentious political issues. A sign out in front of a church in Indianapolis advertised a service at 12:15 p.m. and asked, "How about 15 minutes for God?" Another church I know serves Starbucks and croissants and encourages worshipers to "come as you are. Just *come.*"

When death is near, if you happen to be part of the 66% of the population that doesn't attend worship services regularly, and don't believe in God, it is doubly hard to cope. Consider the predicament. How can you be comforted if you believe that this Life is all there is? Death is nothing but losing a long painful battle. Not surprisingly, Death becomes wild and terrifying.

Thirdly, Technocism. Automakers are pondering putting microwaves and shredders in cars, confirming that there is a profitable niche of auto buyers that continues to be impressed by "bells and whistles." Buyers of these cars may even think about changing their expectations for their car now that it offers these new benefits. They could fix breakfast on the way to work, *in their cars*, for example. They may *literally* make plans to change their life in response to this technology.

As another example, consider how your life has changed through the use of screens that drive the latest consumer and business technologies. From the time you awake until the time you fall asleep at night, your actions are largely dictated by screens. You check your emails on the screen of your home computer. Then it's the screen on your cell phone, your PDA to double-check appointments for the day, the laptop screen at work, the video screen for your remote meetings, and then back to the laptop to order and pay for your lunch on-line. It's all screen-driven technology. You have changed your life to accommodate running your life via screen-based technology.

The way we live teaches us that if we've got a problem that technology can solve, then we really *don't* have a problem. We just haven't found the right technology yet to buy and apply. Remember the story of the Californian who called up NASA wondering if they'd allow him to ride on the space shuttle? Not surprisingly, NASA said no. When he offered them $20 million for the opportunity, their answer changed. Life also teaches us that if we've got enough money, people will work harder to satisfy our desire to access technology. Technology works. The likelihood is that a technology exists *somewhere* to solve any problem. At no time is technology more relevant than at the end of Life. Death forces us to get comfortable with technology because technical innovation and intervention are typical initial responses to terminal diagnoses.

When someone is dying, they and their family become part of the technology revolution immediately. Everybody gets a cell phone so that all know the status of the dying person as well as the doctor's latest comments on their condition. The whole family is surfing the Internet and signing into chat rooms. Medical Specialists with impressive diplomas on their office walls from prestigious universities are hired to dissect and explore the body of the dying person using the latest technologies just in case they can 'solve' the death. The problem: Death cannot be solved.

Finally, Individualism. The largest section in bookstores is the self-help section. Life is so complicated; we believe we need help to be the best we can be. We learn to accept people different than us. We learn the Golden Rule and the value of the individual. Given a terminal diagnosis, though, things change. Death triggers "escalator social stigma" the descent to an all-encompassing, discredited state where Self is valueless.

The dying person becomes absorbed in his own survival, enduring treatments and starting to drop out of Life to preserve what life is left. Too often, the tone of even his closest relationships becomes one of abandonment, because as soon as people learn he is dying, he is no longer treated like part of the living. Even if he doesn't divulge his terminal diagnosis, it becomes evident over time that something is terribly wrong. Friends hesitate to ask, 'What's the matter?" for the same reason they hesitate to visit. They're scared of the randomness of terminal illness and

Death, and know that this could just as easily be happening to them. In facing the death of a friend, they must face their own mortality, and they're not ready to.

The implication is unsettling. The way we die is a reflection of the way we live: both societally and personally. And, in the social framework of Materialism, Secularism, Technocism and Individualism, all of us are ill prepared to die.

Chapter 11

Death Happens

Eighty percent of us are going to die in some kind of healthcare institution, be it a hospital, clinic, hospice, long-term care or nursing home. The problem is that 70% of us don't want to be there. We want to be at home. But families are afraid they don't know how to care for the dying, and worry that the death will happen on their watch. Half of us will die in pain surrounded by strangers. That's the effect of life extending advances such as the intensive care unit. Families think they are doing the best thing they can by holding off Death as long as possible. The problem with depending on life-extension efforts is that Death isn't preventable, and chances are, the person will either be unconscious or among strangers when it happens.

One third of families, because they are desperate for a cure, will bankrupt themselves trying to prevent Death. The reason is understandable: They value Life and are scared of Death. They invest in things they value. Even heroic, expensive efforts to prolong life, however, are not successful in preventing the inevitable.

Even when there is 'warning' of a death by the doctor, often the predictions of patient survival time are woefully inaccurate. Two-thirds of the time, terminal patients' medical directives are ignored because their families cannot bear to enforce them. They don't want their loved one to die before the rest of the family is ready. The doctor may convince the family that more ways of managing the patient's symptoms exist than when the medical directive was signed by the patient. Pursuing new, often experimental therapies, however, typically serves only to drain the pocketbook of the family and the energy of the patient. The 'problem' is not solved, even if symptoms can be curbed.

The expectation of receiving some comfort by the clergy isn't always met either. Some estimates say that up to a third of the clergy are not specially trained to comfort the dying. Instead, their focus is directed primarily to bringing converts to the faith during their lives. Dying patients that do receive some solace say they get a powerful sense of God's love. Many also report the experience of an indescribable peace that comes over them.

My co-founding of the Indianapolis Project on Care of the Dying with Dr. Moller was intended to address some of the failings inherent in the process of death and its aftermath. The Project had four aims:

➢ To educate the clergy on issues related to end-of-life, loss, and grief;
➢ To train a cohort of community volunteers to provide support to individuals and families;
➢ To explore ways in which rituals surrounding the experience of illness, death, funerals, and grief could be made more meaningful; and
➢ To establish a sustainable community-wide network of persons and institutions dedicated to providing caring partnerships for seriously ill persons and their loved ones.

The two-year project jointly funded by Indiana University Medical Center and Batesville Casket Company met each of these goals.

Unfortunately, following the project, the previous scenario reappeared. We learned why: When healthcare, religious, and funeral service professionals formed a caring, collaborative partnership with the dying and their family, spending time with them, dealing with their questions and fears in a truthful and compassionate way, these professionals did so *not* because they would be praised and rewarded by enlightened industries and appreciative individuals, but because they felt, personally, that "it was the right thing to do." With this as the only incentive, enthusiasm and behaviors eventually reverted to the less-demanding ways of the past.

"God's promise was not that life was going to be fair. It was that when we had to confront the pain and the unfairness of life, we wouldn't have to do it alone," explains Rabbi Kushner.

Human Deaths are tragic. Human Deaths, however, are unique among all living things because humans have an *awareness* of the inevitability of Death and of their own Mortality. Lower life forms don't. When a dog runs into the street after the neighborhood cat, he does not know that he is risking his life. By contrast, humans can decide, in many cases, *how* they want to die. Aware of their impending death, they can determine the degree of medical intervention they wish to have, if any. Humans, unlike other living beings, can also *create meaning* about Death and the Life that went before. The flipside of humans' awareness of Death, ability to decide the process of it, and ability to create meaning about it, is that these things also add a level of complexity, suffering and conflict that other living things don't have to deal with. Especially difficult is the conflict, morally and spiritually, that arises in families, as well as in other personal and professional relationships.

When a family member dies, the need for healing shifts to the survivors. They want help but don't know how to ask for it. More than anything, they want their loved one back. That's where funeral service comes in. As one hospice nurse explained it, "When Life ends, the funeral directors take over." Funeral Service runs the final leg of the Death Transition Relay that involves the clergy, the medical community, and the family.

Funerals provide the last opportunity for family members to align themselves and their loved one with Eternity, express their feelings, and move toward closure. For a brief time, a good funeral returns the deceased to loved ones, celebrating their life, wishing them well, and bidding them goodbye. The family, then, is faced with beginning a new reality.

Dying people and their families need help from experts in transitioning from Living, to Life's End, and to a New Beginning. On their own, most don't know where to begin to manage these transitions.

Chapter 12

Funerals and the Media

People watch funerals of the rich and famous on TV, fascinated by how beautiful and personal they are. Then they attend funerals in their hometowns, dismayed by how ordinary and impersonal they are. The impact of this phenomenon for the funeral business is mixed. On the one hand, the public education that occurs about the beauty and poignancy possible with an appropriate funeral is a very positive result. On the other hand, most of the funerals that are held in mainstream U.S.A. bear little resemblance to those beautiful ones seen in broadcasts. Consumers are left feeling that their families do not have access to such ceremonies, and are not entitled to them. The negative result is that the disparity between what is possible and the quality of the funeral they can buy locally gives them reason to believe that the local funerals are valueless.

My own education about funerals began when I was in grade school. The first funeral I ever 'attended' was for President F. Kennedy. I learned that Life comes to a halt when someone dies. School was cancelled so that we could be with our families to 'attend' the funeral. I learned that it is okay to cry when someone dies, even when you don't know the person well. In fact, it seemed like everyone was crying, including my parents and teachers. Even Walter Cronkite was on the verge of tears when little JFK Jr. saluted the passing casket. I learned that funerals are sometimes held outdoors. I learned that the details of the funeral were very important. This funeral had a caisson with a rider-less horse. There were boots facing backward in the stirrups, which signified that the person who died would never return.

Five years after President Kennedy's funeral, Dr. Martin Luther King, Jr. was shot and killed. I was still quite young, and didn't know who Dr. King was, but it was obvious he was very important to a lot of people. I learned that you could learn a lot about somebody just by attending his or her funeral. By the time this one was over, I could appreciate what a horrible tragedy it was that this man had died. His funeral had been very different than President Kennedy's. There was a lot more singing, and there were more speeches by people who worked with Dr. King and shared his beliefs. This funeral was, in some ways, like one final, passionate march against injustice. That made sense for this man and for this ceremony about his legacy.

I was beginning to understand that no two funerals should be the same, because no two people are exactly the same. When Elvis Presley died, I was curious to see what his funeral would be like. This was a man known as *the King*. What sort of funeral do you have for a king whose kingdom reaches around the world? The King's fans felt so very close to him; some felt as if they *knew* him, yet very few people knew him well. I learned that a funeral could satisfy a global audience of admiring strangers and yet be personal enough to comfort a family and close friends at the same time.

Through watching John Lennon's funeral, I learned people would be willing to go to great lengths just to be near the funeral ceremony of someone who had had an enormous effect on their lives. In Lennon's case, that included round-the-clock vigils outside his home at the Dakota, as well as in the streets outside where his funeral was being held. When fellow Beatle, George Harrison died, TV viewers learned about the ritual significance of the Ganges River to the Hindu religion.

By watching the funerals for the Challenger astronauts, we learned what to do when somebody dies at work. First, you focus on the worth of the work they were doing and what it meant to society. Then, you focus on the work team itself, and the fact that each member was well suited for the work. The memorial ceremony for the Challenger Astronauts, though touching as a public tribute to their heroism, was still insufficient as a *personal* tribute, because the astronauts didn't even know each other prior to having been assigned to the mission. Each was a unique individual, whose common link was the work they did together. Because they had separate, private lives, it was appropriate to also have individual funeral ceremonies in their hometowns, to honor them personally.

From Columbine High School, we learned what to do when a number of people are killed, especially when it involves the tragedy of children dying. We learned that people don't want to put a teenager into a casket that looks like one a grandfather was buried in. What they want is something that reflects the vitality of youth. TV viewers wept as they mourned, hoping that someone was helping the families, the school, and the community to cope. The kids themselves taught a nation full of sympathetic viewers about personalized funerals and tributes appropriate for young people. Shrines to the dead appeared at homes, in the school, and at other teen hangouts. The kids wanted to sign the caskets just as they'd sign a yearbook, with funny, poignant, personal messages and promises that they'd never forget the friendship they shared. Typically, funerals don't do that.

When John F. Kennedy, Jr. died, the world learned about cremation and burial at sea. For weeks, authorities tried to locate the doomed airplane and its passengers from the dark waters near Martha's Vineyard. Within days of its recovery, John Kennedy Jr. and his wife were buried at sea with much pomp, poignancy, and ceremony. This sparked quite a bit of conversation and controversy about Catholicism, cremation, and scattering 'ashes' or cremated remains (as the industry calls them). Ted Koppel anchored one notable broadcast on the topic. Because of it, many Catholics learned for the first time that the Catholic Church approves cremation as a form of final disposition. And not only is cremation approved, the *Kennedys* did it. Since, to some, the Kennedys are the closest thing to royalty in the United States, Americans are always curious about the things they do. We believe the Kennedy family's decisions in matters of death and funerals are good ones, because they have had so many experiences with tragedy and untimely death. We suppose that they must know more about the options available than we would. So, we pay attention.

Princess Diana's funeral still stands as the biggest global TV event in history, with 2.5 billion viewers worldwide for the 24-hour continuous broadcast. People watched because of their curiosity about how the legacy of a princess would take shape. What would be said about a life so private in some ways, yet so public in others? Who would decide what mattered most about Diana's life? What things would be said and done, and by whom? After all, this was the last time those who knew Diana best, along with those who admired her from afar, would gather to mourn her, love her, and honor her. Those who watched the funeral will not soon forget when her casket was guided into the cathedral, after having been followed there in procession by her young sons, William and Harry, along with their father Prince Charles, Prince Phillip, and Earl Spencer. What a wonderful, personal touch!

Virtually all Americans experienced the terror of the attacks of September 11, 2001, the grief and anxiety of the year that followed, and all the changes to our way of living. In many ways, that experience taught every human being that when a death occurs, life is never the same again. For most of us, that particular incident did not involve a family member. When death *does* claim a loved one, the impact is intensified. One thing that the 9/11 incident will do is provide a host of information about the importance of the presence of the body of the deceased to the quality of mourning and the journey to closure that the survivors go though. Many of the 9/11 families never got to make that choice. Nearly three thousand people were lost in that tragedy. For 1700 families, no body was available for a funeral ceremony. Their loved ones were cremated involuntarily.

Most ordinary people do not have the opportunity to have as personal and beautiful a funeral as they are accustomed to seeing on television for celebrities. They are not offered the choice to personalize the casket, urn, or service. Instead, they are offered whatever has been customarily provided to people in their communities. That's because their local funeral professional does not believe personalized attention and customization is necessary. They do not believe teaching the community about ritual and mourning is their responsibility. Some believe that they, the funeral director, should be counted on to make any decisions and handle any details the family struggles with. They believe that, for the most part, families know what to do when a loved one dies. But they don't know.

Many of these same funeral directors continue to focus primarily on *tangible* products (caskets, urns, monuments, burial vaults, etc) and traditional services when what their customers want is *intangibles:* funeral details befitting the personality of their loved one, a relationship with an expert they can depend on to advocate and intercede for them, a funeral experience that will be spiritual, fulfilling, intimate, and memorable.

On April 20, 1998, one daughter's anguished lament continued five years after her mother's funeral in a memorial death notice published in *The Houston Chronicle* that read, "I'd like to take this opportunity to apologize for the "generic" funeral we had for Mom five years ago. In my state of shock and grief, I made very bad choices with her funeral."

Chapter 13

The Need for Healing

Recent research reveals that consumers' top three wishes are peace-of-mind, a happy home, and inner bliss. The popularity of affordable methods of looking and feeling better have revealed Americans' impatience with imperfections, and an eagerness to fix things that aren't right, if possible. If consumers' wish is the marketer's command, then marketers must be *healers*.

Many of the world's most noted marketers promise temporary respite and superficial healing from the pressures of Life. The product or service is almost secondary so long as it has a state-of-mind benefit associated with it. Estee Lauder sells a shampoo called Clear Head and 'hope in a bottle' called Peace of Mind.

Gordon's Gin and Tonic promises 'innervigoration'. Reebok makes shoes that do 'mental housekeeping', and American Standard makes 'bathrooms for the soul'. Pepsi introduced drinks named Zen Blend and Karma. Not merely liquid refreshments, mind you, these drinks promise to change your whole aura, baby. Duane Reed Pharmacies offers a line of Bath Therapies. Again, notice that the name itself suggests that just by taking a bath, you can receive healing. Varieties of this product line include Tranquilities, Euphorics, and Healing Garden. All of these examples are indications that our basic human desire for optimal state-of-mind is beginning to rule the dynamics of what motivates and persuades us to buy things.

The urgency to heal what hurts us is so high that spas are even gaining credibility with traditional medicine. The National Institutes of Health says, "Spas are probably doing more than physicians in terms of preventing heart disease." The spa is the perfect atmosphere for mind, body and spirit healing. Indeed, spas are sanctuaries of healing through pleasure.

Spa clients emerge happier, healed, and ready to face the world feeling spiritually and physically whole and refreshed.

Even as opportunities to heal our weary bodies, minds, and spirits proliferate, stress and anxiety are peaking. All told, 96 % of us have made significant changes in our lives in order to relieve increasing mental pressure and stress. Proof is as close as the largest section of the bookstore—Self-help. Most of the book titles there are about stress relief. The CDC and Prevention say that 80% of medical spending is stress-related, and a Harvard professor believes that number could reach 90% soon. Prozac alone has earned Eli Lilly more than $23 billion worldwide. Experts say that many people regularly taking SSRI anti-depressants are actually pursuing optimal state-of-mind. They are not clinically depressed. They say they "feel more like myself," "am becoming someone I like better inside," or "get a better outlook on Life" by taking anti-depressants.

Stress is a culture-inflicted ailment, and healing is our common cultural wish. Funeral directors must understand that consumers' unspoken expectations of them far exceed merely caring for their deceased loved one. Progressive funeral service operators recognize that each family served is in a fragile mental state just by virtue of having endured the anguish of dying, to say nothing about the emotional conflict that funeral planning brings on. The family's need for healing has to be met *first*. Otherwise, their preoccupation with sadness and grief won't let them deal with anything else, no matter what it is (including having meaningful conversations about funeral products and services), or who is asking them.

In a *Wall Street Journal* article in May 2004, Jeffrey Zaslow commented on the next rite of passage for Baby Boomers: burying their parents. In the article, psychologist Bruno Bettelheim observed, "You are not fully an adult until both of your parents are dead."

America's 76 million Boomers (ages 39-58) are losing 4900 of their parents daily. And the numbers of orphaned Boomers will only increase. As caretakers, the Boomers are sustained by their grief as they companion their parents through the stages of dying: denial, anger, bargaining, depression, and finally, acceptance. When death does claim their parents, Boomers' grief turns to mourning, a state-of-mind condition that heals over time. Dr. Alan Wolfelt, a noted thanatologist and grief counselor, defines mourning as "grief gone public." Mourning emerges after death, once a loved one's role changes from caretaker to survivor.

Part of marking the passing of mom and dad and recognizing that 'you're in charge now' is rethinking one's life and career choices and reinterpreting relationships with one's own children. Many Boomers are seeking new ways to keep deceased parents in their lives any way they can, doing their best to accept the fact of their deaths, adapt to it, and then try to move on again toward that elusive goal: optimal state of mind. One of the ways they are trying to heal themselves is by building stronger bonds with their own kids and preparing their own estates in advance of their passing.

Chapter 14

Everything Old is New (and Better)

With all the changes in our lives, our responsibilities, and our world at-large, it's tough to know if we're better off going forward or hunkering down with familiar things that have always worked. It's a puzzling paradox we face daily. We wax nostalgic, but rush to the stores to be first in line to buy the latest thing. We prefer connecting what *has been,* with what *is,* and what *is yet to come.* This is a kinder, gentler, more acceptable way of dealing with change than swearing off the past, present or future altogether. Obviously, denying the necessary changes the future demands is not a choice we can make.

Depending on personal preference, we might choose nostalgia over futurism, and history over progress on a routine basis. More common is the tendency to teeter on the edge of optimism and anxiety. We think we deserve better, so we're willing to take risks, but yearn to remain safe. We indulge in some things while remaining strictly cost-conscious on other purchases. We have an affinity for 'the good old days,' yet want the latest, greatest, futuristic innovations, too. The retro-Thunderbird, for example, earned 'Car of the Year' honors. How gutsy (and inspired) was it for Ford management to dispatch their engineers to have their hand at improving the classic T-bird! Their gamble paid off because the public was delighted with the opportunity to relive their past, *only better.* A similar thing happened when Volkswagen reintroduced the Beetle, *only better,* and when Chrysler introduced the PT Cruiser, a car Elliott Ness of 'The Untouchables' would have loved to drive. Any business, if it intends to be successful year after year, through changes in taste and technology, must be able to reinvent, reorient, retool, and re-staff quickly.

Chapter 15

Class for the Masses

In an impersonal world, the value of unconditional acceptance and 'being included' cannot be underestimated. People want to know that others are ready and willing to help them live the Life they believe they deserve. Today's average consumers have a more sophisticated eye for design and believe they are entitled to the best they can afford. Standards of good taste have been ratcheted upward. The goal of this entitlement fanatic is to constantly improve his or her image. They want to look and live 'mahvelous' in the mainstream, insisting that 'the good life' should be accessible to all. When they get special treatment, they feel important, and conclude that they *matter,* whether they can afford membership into the highbrow country club, or not.

In generations past, if a wealthy customer wanted 'the best money could buy', he sought the oldest provider of what was considered best. Only very few premium quality manufacturers existed, providing the same, high-quality products and services for decades. The problem for such premium quality manufacturers today is that the number of wealthy people who still have a 19th century view of luxury is declining. At one time, these premium quality manufacturers were the only choice for quality-seekers. Now, they are being overlooked by today's wealthy (including well-to-do wannabes), who are choosing to buy from sources they consider to be modern and revolutionary, instead of traditional and classic.

The new entrepreneur's 'in crowd' has replaced what a traditional premium quality manufacturer called 'his customers.' The 'in crowd' is made up of those who wish to participate in forming a new cultural image of what's cool among the privileged. What they select is not at all the same as what old money would choose. The new traditionalists who populate the 'in crowd' demand access to premium products, but are most receptive to manufacturers offering designer styles at low-to middlebrow prices.

New Traditionalists update existing rituals and customs, rewriting the rulebooks containing what appear to them to be arbitrarily rigid, fundamentalist rules. Their interpretation is more modern, practical and personalized. One example is Jordan's Queen Noor. An American who grew up in Minnesota, she married the King of Jordan. The handsome, globetrotting king and queen made Jordan more globally relevant (and hip). The Queen adopted Jordan and its customs as her own. After her husband's death, though, Queen Noor gracefully sidestepped the traditional Jordanian custom in which wives do not attend their husband's funeral. She insisted on attending but remained at a distance from the ceremony. In so doing, she had personalized the traditional custom to her own preference and taste.

The niche of New Traditionalists has been successfully embraced by the cosmetics industry, which was successful in providing class for the masses when they introduced premium department store concepts to supermarkets, superstores, and drugstores. This was another case of smart marketers intent on improving cosmetics consumers' state-of-mind in an increasingly impersonal world, confirming that they *mattered* by offering designer products to them at superstore prices.

More evidence that this approach has great traction with the masses includes the Martha Stewart brand of 380 thread-count sheets available and selling briskly at K-Mart. "Class for the Masses' is the reason why Emeril LaGasse, an ordinary looking guy, can make gourmet cooking seem both masculine and romantic. And, it's why Godiva chocolates sell well at Wal-Mart.

Marketing premium products is no longer a matter of selling what's best to the few, but of selling what's new to the many. Successful marketers of quality goods proactively respond to mainstream demand for what the masses consider to be prestigious. There is strong growth potential for marketers who are in tune with what's hot with new traditionalists. This group, whose ideas catch on quickly, believes their status as 'insiders' allows them to know the newest source of the very latest. In today's marketplace, that's even more important than knowing the oldest source of the very best.

The only possible dark side of providing class for the masses is the confusion it may cause traditional luxury product consumers. When everybody in town has access to the premium products they once had exclusive access to, how can they be sure what really does constitute luxury?

Chapter 16

Life is Fragile

Especially since September 11, 2001, Americans have longed for reassurances that "everything is going to be all right." Without reassurances, Life would be intolerable. In the name of keeping us safe, sane, and reassured, significant changes to our civil liberties have already been made. The silver lining in the painfully tragic events of September 11, 2001 is that it actually helped *grow* our faith and affirm our values. According to a *Woman's Day* poll taken months after the 9/11 attacks, 54% of Americans agreed that Life has meaning and purpose. Two-thirds of Americans agree that just being a witness to the beauty of nature affirms their faith in God.

More compelling is the fact that they said that events involving loss or struggle tend to *affirm* their faith. Nearly six out of ten (57%) say that illness or injury to a loved one strengthens their faith, 55% say the death of a loved one does, and 53% say the September 11th terrorist attacks did. Forty-five percent say that serious illness or injury is something that affirms their faith in God.

Think back to *before* September 11, 2001. We were an American society ambivalent about rituals and freedom, obsessed with work, and largely oblivious to danger. But 9/11 galvanized traditional American values.

September 11, 2001 taught us about diversity not just among Blacks and Whites, but among cultures and continents, too. There were 80 countries represented by the victims in the World Trade Centers.

It taught us about Patriotism. The relief effort activities, blood banks, and community memorials were proof that the nation was willing to dig down deep to help. It also taught us about Tolerance, not just in times of peace, but most critically, at times when suspicion for national security's sake was understandable.

It affirmed that America is one united nation under God. Despite no national religion and a governmental mandate for separation of Church and State, Americans applauded President George W. Bush's suggestion to go to their chosen place of worship and pray.

Through the funerals for the victims, we learned about the importance of Reverence and Respect for Life and Heroes. There were days of national mourning when the stock market was closed, and entertainment and sports events were preempted. American's were unanimous in the belief that the attacks were not something that could or should be ignored, denied or minimized. America knew it needed to begin to heal.

Like no event in recent history, the events of September 11, 2001 sparked an urgent need for human closeness and connection with crowds: family, friends, and like-minded individuals. The activities that coaxed New Yorkers from their homes were going to church, renting movies, and stocking up on comfort food. Book sales, movie attendance, Internet matchmaking and marriages increased, while divorces declined. They longed to belong. Weeks after the attacks, New York neighborhoods reassembled after posting flyers that read, "We are the huddled masses."

Americans have come to the conclusion that to survive the 21st century, meaningful relationships are what will matter most. Some only realize this truth after a life-altering event, or on their deathbed.

Chapter 17

The Crisis of Mistrust

Cynical consumers pledge their loyalty only to institutions, people, and brands they trust. We've moved from a Therapeutic view to a Prophylactic one. In other words, we look longer before leaping into things. In the 1960's, the mantra of the young was, 'If it feels good, do it'. Today, we have a more realistic outlook about the results of such a selfish outlook. We know now that what we do today may be impossible to retract later on.

Our paranoia about being ripped off began in the 1960's with Ralph Nader's Raiders. This prophylactic view is the driving force behind publicly funded government agencies, like the EPA, the FTC, the FDA, and even Homeland Security. These agencies exist to protect us from what we don't know is harmful.

Today, lawmakers and consumers alike are more suspicious and critical of businesses, governments, celebrities and other institutions because of the moral and fiscal corruption of the past few years. The list of companies whose fiscal indulgences and deceptions bilked stockholders and employees out of billions of dollars began with Enron, Arthur Andersen, WorldCom, and Tyco, and seems to lengthen daily. Local businesses, elected leaders and respected community members such as the clergy and teachers have been found to be lacking ethically and morally in recent years. Americans have even encouraged investigative journalists to look for the smoking guns *behind* the story that runs. Without people like Geraldo Rivera, Americans wouldn't know about atrocities in Iraqi prisons now run by Americans. They wouldn't have seen photographs of flag-draped caskets bearing the bodies of American soldiers that the government wanted banned 'out of respect for the families.' They wouldn't know about Bill Clinton, Monica Lewinsky and the tale about cigars that Matt Drudge sniffed out.

The Funeral Rule is just one example of a legal hurdle specifically designed to protect vulnerable consumers from what they don't know might hurt them: Namely, being taken advantage of by deceptive funeral service operations. Certainly, consumers don't want to make quick, costly, irreversible decisions on matters as important as holding an appropriate funeral tribute for their loved one. Even with the Funeral Rule in place, though, when a consumer makes a decision on a funeral that he later regrets, he does not tend to blame himself. Rather, he believes the funeral professional is at fault for allowing the decision to have been made in the first place.

Bottom line, Americans believe they deserve access to as much information as exists. Thanks to an invigorated SEC and FTC, they are getting more, and requiring complete answers to all their questions and concerns before pledging their allegiance to products or politicians. They want product and service guarantees. If their expectations aren't met, they'll demand a refund, accountability and punishment for the guilty.

Those that provide complete customer satisfaction will win trust, business, and loyalty. Those that don't probably won't survive. The many years of denying that personal and organizational integrity had eroded so badly have only strengthened our conviction that we refuse to do business with anyone that isn't completely forthcoming and trustworthy.

Chapter 18

Self Indulgence & Guilt

The truth is that people really don't know what they want. They need help in deciding both what they want and what they need. It is becoming clear that consumer behavior is being ruled by an almost primitive desire that seems as strong as our need for oxygen to breathe.

People act in paradoxical ways. On the one hand, they buy extravagant things because they believe they deserve them. The $1200 suit. The 54" plasma screen they purchased just in time for the Super bowl broadcast. Then, when they get home, they can't explain what came over them to make them feel they needed these extravagances so desperately.

Despite the fact that products in every category are better made than ever, consumers return hundreds of billions of dollars of merchandise each year, having reconsidered whether they really should have bought them in the first place.

We indulge on one hand, and are cost-conscious on the other. According to the book, *The Millionaire Next Door*, a millionaire who achieved that status by shopping at both Saks and Sears heads one-twelfth of American households. In other words, they are discriminating about where they shop and how much they will spend to get what they want.

Chapter 19

Size Matters

With their misgivings about powerful institutions, consumers are more inclined to do business with smaller companies. Changes in smaller businesses are more easily understandable by customers. Small organizations tend to change through innovation, making their products more broadly available, and remaining flexible to serve customer needs.

This mode of consumer thinking is why the funeral service industry will continue to be dominated by small and medium-sized independent firms. Unfortunately, although they have the size advantage, many independent proprietors of funeral homes have seemed adrift. Many saw no need to have a long-term business strategy, believing that the option of selling their firm to larger consolidators would always exist. Then the strategy of the consolidators collapsed because of their miscalculation of the complexity and time it would take to buy, assimilate, operate, and break even with their new acquisitions. To add to the confusion in the market place, leadership among national suppliers was uncertain as a result of jockeying for market position with volume discounts. It became increasingly difficult for the smaller operator to know where to place his trust. The independents hedged their bets, splitting their business between suppliers in an effort not to alienate anyone. It backfired. Long-standing business relationships and loyalties weakened. Ultimately, amid the botched consolidation era, most independent operators stepped back to watch the smoke clear instead of stepping up to aggressively claim market share. Growth opportunities were seized by only the most aggressive, best-funded independents.

Bottom line, though, as long as dealing with small independently owned operations means flexibility and personal attention for consumers, they will continue to prefer them to their larger competitors.

Chapter 20

Women Rule

For the first time, women are realizing their power, using it very effectively, and sometimes just for fun! It's 'take no prisoners' time for the 'weaker' sex. Harley Davidson reports that women are their power customers now. Women are also buying courses in martial arts, and purchasing power tools to build their own homes.

Women are increasingly the decision makers for things that matter commercially, emotionally, physically, and financially. They are the key buyers of, or purchasing agents for, more than half of the gross domestic product of the United States. That means half of all commercial and consumer goods pass muster with women before becoming available to the general public.

Women make three-quarters of all decisions on their family's healthcare. They make more than 90% of decisions on homes, furnishings, medical insurance, and banking. Think about it. When a family gets transferred, the husband says, "Honey I'm supposed to report to work Monday. You go ahead and ride with the real estate agent. You know what kind of neighborhoods we like. Just tell me which driveway to pull into." Why, in so many cases, is the man willing to do this? Because where and how the family lives is *very* important to the woman. It matters, and she wants a say in the decision. Preferably, she'd like to make the call. Judging by the amount of decisions they make, women seem to be making good calls on big purchases.

Today, women account for 46% of the labor force, an increase of close to 60% from the early 1950's. Fifty one percent of women over 35 years old work, and among younger women 16-34, 70% work. The phenomenon of women wielding more commercial and consumer power is not going away, either. For the first time in history, more than half of the freshmen enrolled in American colleges in the fall of 2003 were women. Education researcher Thomas G. Mortensen, who has been calling attention to the gender gap in higher education since the mid-1990's proclaimed victory saying, "Women have won the war in education. It's over with."

Funeral directors ignore women at their own peril. They are the best customer prospects for the industry. The deep faith of American women insists upon ritual and memorialization at Life's end. Larger numbers of women (65% vs. 55% for men) are comforted by religion when times are difficult. A study done by the Center for Gender Equality found that ¾ of American women feel religion is very important in their lives, a number on the increase since 1996. Since women are the ones making the final call on many of the significant family decisions during life, it stands to reason that they would be the ones deciding on products, services and funeral details at Life's end. On end-of-life matters, men defer to their sisters, mothers, or wives.

Among the general population, 54% believe religion is very important. In terms of religious beliefs, and the behaviors that accompany them, though, the female factor stands out. More women than men believe in God and say they are religious, yet more men go to church at least once a week. Is this because women are responsible for kids, elders, and other home front matters that occasionally intervene? With everything else we know about women's lives, probably so.

Women also tend to pray and read religious texts more often. "It is the deep faith of the women of America that calls us to live out the best of what our country stands for. 'In God we trust' is no longer an anachronistic phrase to women. It's very relevant," said the Rev. Dr. Calvin O. Butts III, Pastor of the Abyssinian Baptist Church of New York City.

Religious Beliefs and Behaviors	Men	Women
Consider themselves religious	62%	70%
Believe in God	80%	92%
Pray outside religious services	64%	83%
Read Bible/other religious text	45%	53%
Religion comforts at difficult times	55%	65%
Go to church 1X/week or more	69%	60%

Family Circle Special Survey Report, January 2002

Tom Peters, Uber-guru of business and co-author of the groundbreaking book, *In Search of Excellence*, captured the implication of this trend, saying, "Most businesses just don't get it, or don't *want* to get the fact that women rule. Period." If your company ignores women, then they will ignore your company first as an employer, and then as a customer.

Chapter 21

Stages of Consumer Behavior

When the pioneer of the death-awareness movement, Elisabeth Kubler-Ross, brought Death into the mainstream of polite conversation in 1969, and described the inescapable, progressive stages of dying: Denial, Anger, Bargaining, Depression, and finally Acceptance, she couldn't have known that those very same stages quite accurately describe the nature of 21st Century human behavior.

What Kubler-Ross called Denial parallels today's search to dodge the pressures of reality in escapist experiences.

Anger is today's acting-out behavior such as road-rage tantrums and violence in schools and work places. Culturally, we even *organize* our anger in civil demonstrations. Hundreds of websites call for boycotts or publish the grievances of ticked-off consumers.

Bargaining is what we do to cut the best deal possible with a Higher Power, hoping and praying for a simple, supernatural healing of our pain.

Depression lines up with our disappointment in our physical reality and fear of the future. Acceptance is belief in the premise of an invisible, omnipotent being who controls it all. The alternative to Acceptance, that this Life is all there is, certainly isn't comforting by comparison.

Chapter 22

Spirituality Yes, but is it Religion?

Indeed, there has been an upsurge in spirituality. Our heavenward yearning began in the late 1990s, when *Time* magazine featured an angel on its cover and an article touting meditation, Zen Buddhism, New Age Thinking and celebrations of simple abundance. Yoga, t'ai chi, herbal tea and feng shui were recommended. It was 'religion *lite*'.

In a national survey conducted just a few months after the September 11, 2001 attacks, more than 2/3 of respondents (68%) claimed to be religious. Almost one third (32%) said they are not religious.

The word 'religious' appears to mean different things to different people. Even though more than half the population believes religion is important, that doesn't necessarily mean that there has been a corresponding rise in conventional religious behavior. More than a third of those identifying themselves as religious (36%) said they do not belong to a church, synagogue, or other religious community, and more than 2/3 of those who said they are not religious (68%) said they believe in God. This has given rise to a phenomenon some refer to as "the church with just one pew." What this means is that if something is inherently spiritually satisfying, then it doesn't matter what mainline religion thinks about it. The broader definition of 'religious' must be catching on. The loss in membership by organized, mainstream religions appears to have been the gain of this new spirituality of 'altered states'.

Some of these new religions are re-stages of the old ones, some are all new versions of them, and some are completely new. All offer improved ways to achieve a mystical, perceptible, psycho-spiritual experience. More evidence that imaginational experiences are paramount in spirituality: the fastest growing religion today is evangelical-rock Christianity. And the largest portion of today's new churches are Gospel churches.

This upswing in non-traditional religious observance is probably driving the increase in requests for more experiential funeral rituals. For those seeking a powerfully personal spiritual experience, it is not enough for God to heal their pain silently. They want to *feel* the power of the supernatural, and have the spirit inside them. In short, they want the religious *experience*, not just the result.

Chapter 23

God is Back

Positive power comes from Faith in God: Religious people seem to be more optimistic than non-religious people. Religious people believe good will triumph over evil (77% vs. 46% for the non-religious), everything happens for a reason (80% vs. 65%), and love conquers all (67% vs. 53%).

Even after experiencing a Death, religious people interpret events in ways that strengthen their beliefs, not shatter them. There is something inexplicably comforting in having a faith to rely on, especially in difficult circumstances; such as death (your own or someone else's). The Bible promises "the peace that passes all understanding." Even this is an invitation to consumers to achieve optimal state-of-mind just by becoming a Christian.

Ninety-one percent of Americans say they believe in miracles, according to Gallup Polls, and nearly half that (47%) say they've witnessed one. 82% say prayer heals, and medical studies have proven that the combination of prayer and positive spirituality significantly improves cure rates. Ninety-three percent of Americans say they believe in God, a number that has remained unchanged since the 1990's. Those who believe in God-related things such as angels (72%), the Devil (65%), Heaven (87%), and the ability to be in Heaven after death (93%), have all increased.

For a long time, any overt expressions of religiosity were seen as unnecessary, un-cool, or un-called for. In the 1970's, President Jimmy Carter's humility in admitting that he had committed adultery in his heart, but not in actuality, was seen as a weakness and a political liability. Contrast that to more recent public evidence that it's become hip to be God-fearing.

The moral and religious mettle of President Bill Clinton came under fire when he was discovered to have lied about having a sexual liaison with White House intern Monica Lewinsky. The initial response of President George W. Bush to terrorist attacks against the U.S. on September 11, 2001 was to ask all Americans to pray. Americans not only complied but also applauded him for his wisdom in addressing this sensitive world-changing situation with an appeal to the mercy of God. We flocked to mosques, cathedrals, churches, temples, and synagogues, and prayed for guidance. Halfway around the world, Bush's ally Tony Blair also made public declarations about his faith that helped him win the post of British Prime Minister.

At former president Ronald Reagan's state funeral in June of 2004, Baroness Margaret Thatcher, former President George H.W. Bush, and George W. Bush all invoked God and Jesus Christ in their remarks about Reagan's legacy to the country and the world. Reverend John Danforth, the funeral celebrant at the National Cathedral, announced upfront that the memorial service would be about Christ-based faith as much as it was about Reagan, the man. Given the traditionally ecumenical nature of events held at the National Cathedral, this was a surprise. In fact, the theme of the funeral was appropriately based on the Sermon on the Mount. In Life, Reagan often invoked imagery of the "City on the Hill" when referring to the promise and responsibility of America. Orchestrated as it was around the "City on the Hill" theme, Reagan's intimate, personal funeral was tastefully matched to his life and legacy.

Chapter 24

Storytelling

Consider the amount of attention given lately to the concept of personal brand image: the increasing popularity of cosmetic surgeries, the importance of how we present ourselves to potential employers, colleagues, lovers, and others in Life. Personhood, a.k.a. personal brand image, is built throughout one's life, by stories. Resumes, for instance, are summaries of the stories relevant to our professional lives.

Stories work. Jesus used simple stories to impart lessons, explain concepts, and assure people of divine comfort and guidance. Stories are instructive. Parables clarified his teaching, making it easier for people to see applications of divine truths in their daily lives. Particularly when a loved one dies, survivors are confused and feel abandoned. At such times, sound bites and maxims just don't satisfy their probing, questioning, searching hearts.

Even in the commercial market place, stories have begun to replace slogans as a way to sell products and build brand image. BMW films hires A-list directors such as Ang Lee and Guy Ritchie to produce short movies that will generate more traffic on its website. The company also invests aggressively in product placement for James Bond movies. Everyone knows Bond drives a BMW, don't they? Bulgari Jewelers also realized the power of using non-traditional means of telling the story of their fine jewelry. Instead of investing in traditional media and 30-second commercials, they grabbed the spotlight by commissioning Fay Weldon; a British author, to write a novel whose plot would inject mythology and mystery into the experience of Bulgari. The plan worked and the book became a hot seller—with Bulgari jewelry as the star.

For the funeral service industry, the ability to retell a person's life story through tales that inform, captivate and entertain is critical. At the end of life, people don't just want to know somebody lived and now they don't. They want to linger and savor the life that was lived through stories of the experiences of that life. Maybe that's why autobiographical writing classes designed to encourage capturing memories for posterity's sake, are growing in popularity among the elderly. They want stories to be re-told at their funerals. People approach Death, and consider having a funeral, they dwell on whether the Life they lived is worth telling stories about. In fact, that becomes the crux of the issue. Is there any reason to retell the story of their Life experiences? And, if so, who should shoulder the task of deciding what mattered to this person and to their survivors about that person? Who ought to author, orchestrate and host this storytelling celebration of Life? It's a huge responsibility that the funeral director hopes he or she gets to take on.

Whether a family chooses to memorialize a loved one, and how good the funeral is that results has *everything* to do with the power of the life story.

If telling stories as a method of increasing consumers' interest in funerals seems too odd to embrace, you're not alone. Peter Drucker, a world leader in leadership and management, says, "The reason most organizations don't respond well to change is not that they don't see the need to change and adapt, but that they spend almost all of their resources on trying to preserve the past." He surely would have gained the agreement of genius Albert Einstein, who observed, "The significant problems we face cannot be solved at the same level of thinking we were at when we created them."

Part II
What to Do

Chapter 1

Grow or Else

Businesses must commit to pursuing continual growth or face the fate of the buggy whip. Organizations and markets change based on where they are in a three-stage growth model. The three stages are the Formative, Normative, and Integrative stages. In the formative stage, companies are in startup mode, highly motivated, productive and profitable. Their mission is to seek out buyers and gain loyal users. As the market matures, potential competitors realize they could also profit from meeting customer needs just as the pioneering firm has. But the entry of each new competitor to the market means increased price competition because new firms must pillage market share from the leader while (hopefully) innovating to attract interest among new prospects. Finally, the Integrative phase arrives when the market has become fully saturated. By now, competition has sucked the profitability out of the business. As former GE CEO Jack Welch said, "If you can't sell the world's greatest product at the world's lowest price, you're going to be out of business." At no time is his advice truer than at the Integrative stage. That is the current stage of funeral service. Unless meaningful, consumer-relevant innovations are introduced, the funeral service industry as we know it will continue to slow down and decline as it matures. In its natural decline, it will take profitability and customers with it.

Chapter 2

Personalize

Look around. There is no mass market anymore. No single way to accomplish something. No one offer with universal appeal. This is true even of the fact that everyone will someday die. Yes, we will all die, but that doesn't mean we'll all do it the same way, or want the same sendoff. The meaning of life for each person is unique. Everything about the death, dying and funeral experience ought to be negotiable, customizable, and personal. The social values of materialism, secularism, technocism, and individualism will have made all of us ill equipped to die, but for different reasons. Desire for some measure of control in this unsupportive world leads us to want to be treated like the individuals we are.

Personal assistants are now being hired by whole communities to help individual households with everything from shopping, to holiday decorating and cooking, to party planning and even funeral planning. An offshoot of this desire for personal attention, stress relief, and convenience is the increased popularity of anything packaged to meet specific needs. Packaged funerals, for instance.

Chapter 3

Educate your customers

The rapidly expanding elder population demands more attention and knowledge. Their experience with every other consuming experience leading up to a death has been one of increasing levels of customer service. They receive everything from senior discounts, to virtual ordering and immediate delivery to 24/7/365 hot lines, to customization. These consumers want to make good decisions about important end-of-life matters. Funeral Directors need to help them navigate this scary terrain. Even if an elderly consumer believes in the value of memorializing a loved one, he or she will need to be educated as to options for doing so, and at a time when he or she will be overwhelmed emotionally and often financially following months and perhaps years of chronic illness.

Chapter 4

Be the Chooser

We approach death the way we approach Life, by choosing mentors to advise us. We pick Oprah to tell us who is worth listening to, and what the social issues of the day are. We trust her to select the books we read. We count on her to select upstanding charities for her Angel Network so that we can send her our loose change to help. We've trusted Richard Branson; a gifted marketer with a high school education who founded Virgin Airways by scribbling on a blank sheet of paper a vision for what airline travel ought to be like. Consumers remained intrigued with Branson's ideas as he pursued the music industry, successfully founding Virgin Mega Stores without any previous experience in that industry. With each successful venture, he proves that his ideas are worth paying attention to, and that he is worth choosing to serve us, whether it is on an airline flight or in our CD buying experience. We put more and more faith in people like Branson each time they suggest to us what it is we want, promise our satisfaction, and then deliver for us.

When Wal-Mart began its quest to become the nation's largest retailer, it proceeded methodically, approaching leading manufacturers in key categories about making its private label products. That means, as a consumer, you can be quite certain that leading manufacturers are producing Sam's Choice items to exacting specifications. By letting Wal-Mart choose for you, you receive the state-of-mind benefits of convenience and time saving because you avoid having to be concerned with dissecting the claims of competing national brands.

In funeral service, the role of chooser is there for the taking. This role would involve a position of authority on all matters related to the end-of-life, including more than just funeral planning. This chooser would advise, package, and simplify decisions for consumers overloaded with grief and burdened with logistical details. Life itself is complex. Death adds to the loneliness and confusion and subtracts familiar sources of comfort and support. The vision, expertise, and service minded-ness of a Funeral Service Authority could be the solution.

Chapter 5

Be a Healer

We've been caught up in the lure of attaining instant altered states. Even smart marketers who are aware of the 'healer' strategy struggle with customers' demand for relief *right now.*

The demand for new ways to manage Life is intensifying. Accordingly, growth is possible for businesses offering new ways to simplify Life. The search for optimal state-of-mind means funeral service professionals must revisit the benefits of their products and services. In particular, they need to educate consumers about the therapeutic, healing benefits of holding a funeral. Escaping Death is impossible, but funeral service professionals can become trusted companions on the journey of mourning, if they are able to convince consumers that they provide relief and healing.

Chapter 6

If you do it, Brand it

Every industry believes that as soon as more than one competitor exists, their products and services are endangered by commoditization (the perception that what they do is not unique, but something that anybody can do, at any number of price points). To be sure, it's necessary to constantly reaffirm the relevancy and value of your products and services. Your product has to improve people's lives, and the experience you provide in offering that product has to be surprising, indulgent, and so exceptional your customers want souvenirs to remind themselves about it.

A shift has occurred in the market place: from selling things to buying things. For example, today, customers can buy stocks over the Internet without dealing with a salesperson or broker. They can also buy caskets and urns without dealing with a licensed funeral director. When products and services are bought rather than sold with the recommendation of a salesperson, consumers make their purchase decisions based on their knowledge of brands.

The brand 'pre-sells' the product or service. A branding program develops the consumer perception that your product and service offerings are different, and better, than the others. The trick for funeral directors is to connect the broader state-of-mind benefits of the funeral with the power of their brand.

Benefits carry much more weight when they are structured around the brand's credentials. When a sunscreen claims to prevent sun damage to the skin, for instance, the claim is more credible if it comes from the best-selling brand. Nearly every firm can find some credentials that it can publicize. And, if not, it can create the credentials by inventing a new category. That is exactly what many funeral homes are doing by opening lavish facilities for events. This broadens their appeal and gives them a unique credential their competitors cannot match. It does not detract from their funeral service operation. It enhances it. Other things that work in building brands successfully are:

1. Cultural relevancy: Make sure the things you do matter to your customers.
2. Consistency between visual and verbal cues. In other words, be what you seem to be. Dress the part.
3. The value in belonging. This isn't about price/value relationships. This is about conveying what the brand *believes* to its users, implicitly gaining their agreement, and becoming part of their value system instead of occupying a narrow part of their life.

Branding in the funeral service sector must expand its appeal to both religious and secular consumers. Poignancy and meaningful services and ceremony are not dependent on one's views on the existence of a Higher Power. In fact, with the growth in popularity in unconventional religious observance, requests for something 'different' or 'non-traditional' will increase.

Both for mature brands and relatively new ones, the key factors in the ability to survive in a competitive marketplace will be the ability to reinvent, reinterpret their benefits, and reorient their marketing campaigns to changing consumer demographics. That doesn't mean the brand must deny its heritage or authenticity. Just that a brand's usefulness and relevancy must change over time

Chapter 7

Speed up Service

We want what we want. We want it customized, and we want you to confirm that we're going to get it when we want it. Guaranteed. Anything not immediate is slow. In fact, more and more, our loyalty to brands is dictated not by the brand's quality, but by immediacy and access. This desire for immediacy is strongly related to consumers' desire for control in a world gone crazy. Think for a moment about the standard of good service for consumer durables: appliances or automobiles, for instance. Same day service. Free delivery. Pricing terms. Free financing. 24-hour free test-drives. Given these delightful experiences on high-priced products, it's natural for us to expect fast, customized, reliable service by *all* members of any company.

The Internet has spoiled us because, with it, everything is immediate. We gripe about additional seconds it takes to load the information we wish, but still use it as an important source for answers to all our questions. The Internet, then, ought to have a role in all plans for your firm, including recruiting, communications, education, sales support, and 24/7/365 customer service.

Chapter 8

Offer end of life benefits

It is no secret that Americans are getting older and living longer, but fewer than 25% of companies offered eldercare benefits in 1998. Still, that number is growing, having doubled since 1990. Employers now estimate that 20 to 30% of their employees are caring for parents, requiring them to be preoccupied and absent more often. Aetna reports that it has saved three dollars in better productivity and reduced absenteeism for every dollar it spends on eldercare benefits. A study done for Metropolitan Life Insurance Company backed up that level of saving and went further, saying that employers save $3-$5 for each dollar they invested in helping employees find eldercare resources.

When Fortune profiled America's best companies in 2003, number 16 on their list was Vision Service Plan, located in Rancho Cordova, California. VSP converted an enormous fountain in front of its corporate headquarters to a memorial for deceased former employees. The idea began with a suggestion to the CEO from a grieving employee whose co-worker had recently died. "When I heard the request, the light went on in my mind that all of these persons were good people for us," said CEO Roger Valine, a 29 year company veteran himself. This is a unique, personalized benefit and a powerful recruiting tool, because existing and prospective VSP employees have tangible evidence that they matter to the company. The vitality and success of the company is *literally* part of the legacy of everyone who ever worked there.

Chapter 9

Champion awareness, prevention, and preparation

The health care industry has led the way on building awareness of the inevitable. Men's lower life expectancy and women's decision making power led the medical community to conclude that generating more awareness of diseases that often strike the elderly could improve detection and cure rates. It certainly has struck a chord with the public, no matter how delicate the subject matter is. Remember a couple of years ago, when Bob Dole was talking about Viagra on the Super Bowl broadcast, and the public seemed to emit a collective gasp because he was talking about erectile dysfunction? Times have changed. In 2004, advertisers paid $2.3 million for a thirty second commercial in the Super Bowl broadcast. *Seven* thirty second commercials advertising prescription drugs for erectile dysfunction ran. *The Wall Street Journal* wondered the following day if the broadcast should have been re-named the Erectile Dysfunction Bowl. Now the door has been flung open on what used to be considered delicate subjects, conversations have intensified about several other common diseases of the elderly. It's not just erectile dysfunction any more. Now it's also prostate cancer, and Alzheimer's. And the heroic and famous are pitchmen, including Arnold Palmer, Andy Grove, Norman Schwarzkopf, and Charleton Heston.

Think about the value for funeral directors in championing the preparations necessary for end-of-life decisions. Consumers don't just need to be pre-plan their funerals. End of Life advice from the 'Meaning of Life' Authority ought to include wellness in every area of consumers' lives. That means helping them make informed decisions about Life, Love, Learning, Laughing (enjoyment), and Legacy (personal and financial).

Chapter 10

Create Desire

Our most basic urges and desires drive our actions. For marketers, understanding what's at the root of consumer urges and desires leads to product and service solutions that scratch the *real* consumer itch, meeting the heart's desire head-on.

Simply claiming that only premium quality goods are sold by the company is not enough. Premium is in the eye of the beholder. Premium quality may qualify a funeral home for consideration by the family but does not ensure that it will win them as a customer. For that, they must see your firm playing a major role in meeting their heart's desire.

I've said that people only buy what they believe they need to help improve their life. For funeral service to remain viable, consumers must perceive its value to them *personally*. They must *want* to participate in memorialization activities. The industry needs to demonstrate its expertise in hosting ceremonies of all types that prove it can accommodate whatever requests they receive.

Buchanan Group built its Community Life Center at Washington Park East Cemetery in Indianapolis to expand its presence beyond its successful funeral service operations. The spectacular 20,000 square foot facility now hosts political debates, community groups, and the monthly Rotary Club luncheon. One measure of the community's acceptance of Buchanan Group's expanded service is the fact that more than a hundred weddings have been held at the facility, which has only been in operation for three years.

When it comes to end of life decisions, people don't want to make quick decisions they will someday regret. Creating desire means consumers should understand the benefits of funerals, as well as the consequences of *not* having one. They should know whether planning and experiencing a funeral will matter to their healing tomorrow, a year from now or 20 years from now. They should come to appreciate that Mourning is the beginning of Healing. And those that mourn well heal well.

Chapter 11

Stage Experiences

We process Life through a series of stories we tell. It doesn't matter if the stories are true or not. Thanksgiving wouldn't be the same at many homes if the same family stories were not told year after year. Stories simply make Life more interesting by providing meaning and mythology. One aspect of our search for the spiritual mountaintop is the desire for stories that stimulate the senses, provide hope & enlightenment, and get us closer to our optimal state of mind.

The reason why "It's a Wonderful Life" is so resonant for all of us; the reason we watch it over and over, is that it is a story about the unique value of one irreplaceable man's life. George Bailey receives a wonderful gift—the opportunity to see what Life would have been like had he never been born. Sure, it's a Frank Capra fantasy. But the popularity of Frank Capra films is the fact that they captivate and engage and enthrall. It matters not that the story is a fantasy; we want to believe it is true. We almost will it to be true because its message assures us that our own lives are not lived in vain. This movie encourages us to live gratefully, even during the difficult times.

A funeral that tells stories that teach, entertain, encourage emotion, transformation and participation taps into all of the senses. The décor of the funeral home, the lighting design, memory boards and scrapbooks and all the elements of personalization delight the eye of the beholder, while the music used, the sound system quality, the readings selected, and the performance of the narrators, speakers, and celebrants delight the ear. The feel of the seating and the loft of the carpeting, the sensory experience of touching the casket, urn, statuary, flowers, and even the quality of the paper stock used in the program can be nurturing or nothing at all. The food at the reception following the service literally feeds the sense of taste. And the fragrance of flowers, candles, and incense address the sense of smell, which, incidentally, is the sense most closely associated with memories and emotion. Familiar fragrances or smells associated with the ritual or the loved one should be critical strategic elements in planning memorable funerals that reflect the life of the deceased.

This ability to create the story of a lifetime for every family will be a critical skill to fortify the future of the funeral service industry. Absent this ability, the industry's purpose and value to consumers is questionable.

Chapter 12

Talent=Money

You've got to be a talent scout. Look at how professional sports teams operate. These organizations are dependent on selling tickets and entertaining fans. Putting on a good show and winning games & championships is one way to do that. They must also pay attention to which players they hire to be on the team. Each year, those organizations review their rosters and decide whether the right people are in place to entertain and to win games. If too many players with redundant skill sets are on the team, management trades those they don't need. Then, they replace those players with skills in other areas that need to be strengthened, so that the team will improve its entertainment value, sell more tickets and have a better chance at winning championships. Management searches for professionals in any number of places, including on competing teams, in other sports, and now in high schools around the world.

Within the funeral service industry, as with all others, professional renewal must be everyone's task. Successful organizations have the ability to reinvent themselves in response to the market, to re-staff and re-tool as necessary, and to redesign their game plan to remain competitive.

In the search for the elusive 'franchise players' for your business, don't insist on technical skills in mortuary science as a prerequisite. Understand that, having experienced a death in the family, families don't have any knowledge of your company's talent for embalming. Most often, a funeral home is not selected because of a reputation for embalming any more than McDonald's is chosen for lunch because they cook hamburgers. These business fundamentals (embalming for a funeral home, and cooking hamburgers for a fast-food restaurant) are merely the price of entry. They *must* be done and they must be done *well*. Yet, excellent fundamentals alone will not ensure your success, although they may get you a spot on the consumer's radar screen along with a slew of other places they could select. The reason consumers decide to shop you or buy from you is *beyond* the fundamentals. What *else* do you provide?

Often the most progressive funeral service firms hire people with no specific skills in the industry, but with relevant experience, coach-ability, and awesome potential. Your firm must offer more than fundamentals; beyond that, the additional benefits must be relevant and desirable to consumers. They could include the interpersonal skills of your staff, their creativity, helpfulness and resourcefulness, organizational skills, or their ability to plan and host memorable events. It *must* be something, however, that the *consumer* values, and it may be something you don't offer them . . . yet.

Chapter 13

Forget on purpose

Always be looking for new ways to arrive at 'aha!' moments. Remember, funeral service is a vocation that is about something bigger than you. In a very real sense, it's about keeping you and Humanity one with the universe forever.

Purposeful forgetting doesn't mean to be disorganized. You must remain organized, while remaining *strategically* forgetful. That may mean doing things differently just so that you can benefit from the learning that *could* happen, and the discoveries you *might* stumble upon. Avoiding what is familiar is as easy as taking a different route home from work. In the process, you learn new streets, neighborhoods, stores, and communities. You may meet new people

If there were no policies or procedures for your business, how would you act? What would you do that you believe would have terrific results? Pretend that you have no previous experience in this industry. What do you think people would want from you? What do you think people need? What do you think would move them closer to their optimal state-of-mind? Go ahead and try some new processes and approaches. The simplest, best skill you can develop as a leader is forgetting what has been done before. Think of what ought to be done now. Funeral Service is not an industry that merely takes care of the dead. At its best, it is an industry that defines the meaning of Life and clarifies legacies for every family it serves.

Do these things, and consumers will insist on dealing with you not because you are *one* of the best funeral homes they could choose, but because *you are the only one who does what matters most.*

Bibliography

Bernstein, Elizabeth. "Do it Yourself Religion." *The Wall Street Journal.* June 11, 2004

Davis, Melinda. "The New Culture of Desire." The Free Press. 2002

Dychtwald, Ken. "Age Power." Jeremy P. Tarcher/ Putnam. 1999

"Eldercare Tasks Cost Business $11 Billion a Year: Workplace Programs Can Bring Significant Reduction." *Employee Benefit Plan Review.* September 1997

Employee Benefit Research Institute. "Databook on Employee Benefits." Washington, DC EBRI, 1997

LaSalle, Diana and Britton, Terry A. "Priceless." HBS Press. 2003

Levering, Robert and Moskowitz, Milton. "100 Best Companies to Work For." *Fortune Magazine. January 20, 2003*

Matathia, Ira & Salzman, Marian. "Next." The Overlook Press. 1999

Moller, David. "Life's End." Baywood Publishing Company. 1999

Moller, David "Confronting Death." Oxford University Press. 1996

U.S. Bureau of the Census. Current Population Reports, Series P23-194 Population Profile of the United States, 1997. Washington DC GPO, 1998

Wallace, Gini Kopacky. "In God We Trust." *Woman's Day Magazine.* January 15, 2002

Wolfelt, Alan. "Creating Meaningful Funeral Experiences." Companion Press. 2003

Printed in the United States
23888LVS00001B/343

9 781413 463316